RUSSIA

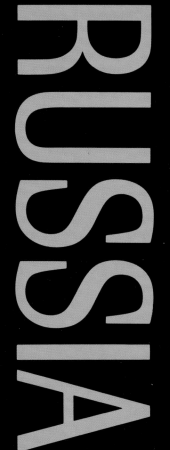

RUSSIA

THEN & NOW

Prepared by
Geography Department

Lerner Publications Company
Minneapolis

Series editors: Mary M. Rodgers, Tom Streissguth,
  Colleen Sexton
Photo researcher: Bill Kauffmann
Designer: Zachary Marell

Our thanks to the following people for their help in
preparing and checking the text of this book: Dr. Craig
ZumBrunnen, Department of Geography, University of
Washington; Sergej Schachowskoj.

Pronunciation Guide

Arkhangelsk	ahr-KAN-gelsk
glasnost	GLAZ-nost
Nizhni Novgorod	NIZH-nee NAHV-geh-rahd
Nikita Khrushchev	nyik-YEE—TUH kroosh-CHAWF
Okhotsk	oh-KAHTSK
perestroika	pehr-eh-STROY-kah
Pskov	pih-SKAHF
sukhoveys	soo-koh-VEES
Voronezh	vuh-RAH-nish
Urals	YOOR-als

Words in **bold** type are listed in a glossary that starts on page 60.

LIBRARY OF CONGRESS CATALOGING-IN-PUBLICATION DATA

Russia / prepared by Geography Department, Lerner Publications
  Company.
       p. cm. — (Then & now)
    Includes index.
    Summary: Discusses the topography, ethnic mixture, history,
and current political situation of Russia, the largest republic in
the former Soviet Union.
    ISBN 0-8225-2805-3 (lib. bdg.)
    1. Russia—Juvenile literature. [1. Russia.] I. Lerner Publica-
tions Company. Geography Dept. II. Series: Then & Now
(Minneapolis, Minn.)
DK17.R864 1992
947—dc20   92-7833
                                                 CIP
                                                  AC

Manufactured in the United States of America
1 2 3 4 5 6 97 96 95 94 93 92

• CONTENTS •

INTRODUCTION • 7

CHAPTER ONE
The Land and People of Russia • 11

CHAPTER TWO
Russia's Story • 29

CHAPTER THREE
Making a Living in Russia • 43

CHAPTER FOUR
What's Next for Russia? • 55

GLOSSARY • 60

INDEX • 63

In west central Russia, two girls play with their cat on a farm in the foothills of the Ural Mountains.

"Russia is always defeated but never beaten."

Old Russian Saying

In 1992, the Soviet Union would have celebrated the 75th anniversary of the revolution of 1917. During that revolt, political activists called **Communists** overthrew the czar (ruler) and the government of the **Russian Empire.** The revolution of 1917 was the first step in establishing the 15-member **Union of Soviet Socialist Republics (USSR).**

The Soviet Union stretched from eastern Europe across northern Asia and contained nearly 300 million people. Within this vast nation, the Communist government guaranteed housing, education, health care, and lifetime employment. Communist leaders told farmers and factory workers that Soviet citizens owned all property in common. The new nation quickly **industrialized,** meaning it built many new factories and upgraded existing ones. It also modernized and enlarged its farms. In addition, the USSR created a huge, well-equipped military force that allowed it to become one of the most powerful nations in the world.

By the early 1990s, the Soviet Union was in a period of rapid change and turmoil. The central

Fireworks light up the sky above the Kremlin in Moscow, the Russian capital. Once the headquarters of the Soviet Union, the Kremlin now houses the governmental offices of independent Russia.

government had mismanaged the economy, which was failing to provide goods. To control the various ethnic groups within the USSR, the Communists had long restricted many freedoms. People throughout the vast nation were dissatisfied. In response, the Soviet government allowed open elections in Russia, the largest Soviet republic. In the summer of 1991, Russian voters chose Boris Yeltsin, who had resigned from the Communist party, as president of Russia.

At the same time, several other republics were seeking complete independence from Soviet rule—a development that worried some old-style Communist leaders. In August, these conservative Communists tried to use Soviet military forces to overthrow the president of the USSR. Led by Yeltsin, thousands of Russian citizens opposed to this action blocked streets in Moscow, the nation's capital. Within a few days, the attempted overthrow had

In Siberia—a vast region of woodlands and plains that covers northern, southern, and eastern Russia—vendors display their flowers in the city of Krasnoyarsk.

failed, which hastened the breakup of the Soviet Union.

A few months later, Russia formed the **Commonwealth of Independent States** with several other former Soviet republics. By far the largest and most populous member of this commonwealth, Russia possesses a wealth of natural resources, huge tracts of fertile land, and a powerful military. It remains the dominant state among the 11 former Soviet republics now in the commonwealth.

Russian leaders are attempting to improve the economy of their nation by freeing prices and by allowing private businesses to operate. Mismanagement within the country, however, is slowing economic recovery. In addition, conflict among Russia's many different ethnic groups threatens to divide the nation at an important time. Although Russia has made a clear break with its past, its future remains uncertain.

A female figure symbolizing "Mother Russia" dominates a World War II memorial in Volgograd (formerly Stalingrad). This city in southwestern Russia suffered great destruction during fierce fighting between Germans and Russians in 1942 and 1943.

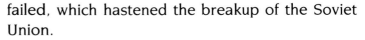

Friends push a homemade go-cart down a sidewalk in Moscow.

CHAPTER ONE

The Land and People of Russia

The vast territory of Russia covers more than 6.5 million square miles (17 million square kilometers). This area is more than twice the size of the United States. The Ural Mountains divide the country into European (western) and Asian (eastern) regions. At its easternmost point, Russia lies only 50 miles (80 km) from the state of Alaska across the Bering Strait.

• Topography and Rivers •

European Russia—most of which is made up of flat, treeless plains known as **steppes**—borders several former Soviet republics. Kazakhstan lies to the southeast, and Ukraine is in the southwest. Belarus, Latvia, and Estonia are west of Russia. Finland's long border with Russia runs from the Gulf

Cross-country skiers race to the finish of a marathon in the northwestern city of Murmansk.

Tall grasses and wildflowers cover the treeless Siberian steppes (plains) in southern Russia.

of Finland in the south to the Barents Sea, an arm of the Arctic Ocean, in the north.

Southern Russia rises to the Caucasus Mountains, which form the Russian frontier with the newly independent states of Georgia and Azerbaijan. These lands lie between two large inland seas—the Black Sea and the Caspian Sea. In the east, the vast Russian territory of Siberia covers the northern half of the Asian continent—from the Arctic Ocean in the north to Kazakhstan, Mongolia, and China in the south.

Siberia itself consists of a northern belt of **tundra**—permanently frozen, treeless plains—and a vast coniferous (evergreen) forest known as the **taiga.** The forest stretches from northwestern Russia to the Bering Sea, an arm of the Pacific Ocean. Farther south along the Pacific coast are the Sea of Okhotsk, Sakhalin Island, the Kuril Islands, and the Sea of Japan, which separates the Russian mainland from Japan.

Autumn foliage frames one of the spires of the Peter and Paul Fortress in the northwestern city of St. Petersburg.

Russia contains several of the world's longest rivers. In European Russia flows the wide Volga River, which passes a series of dams, canals, and industrial cities before emptying into the Caspian Sea. In Siberia, the Ob, Yenisei, and Lena rivers are important transportation routes that flow north to the Arctic Ocean. The Amur River forms Russia's border with northeastern China. Lake Baikal, the world's deepest lake, lies in southern Siberia near the Mongolian border. Recent conservation efforts have been aimed at preserving the lake's unique environment.

A farmer transports food for his livestock across the Volga River in western Russia.

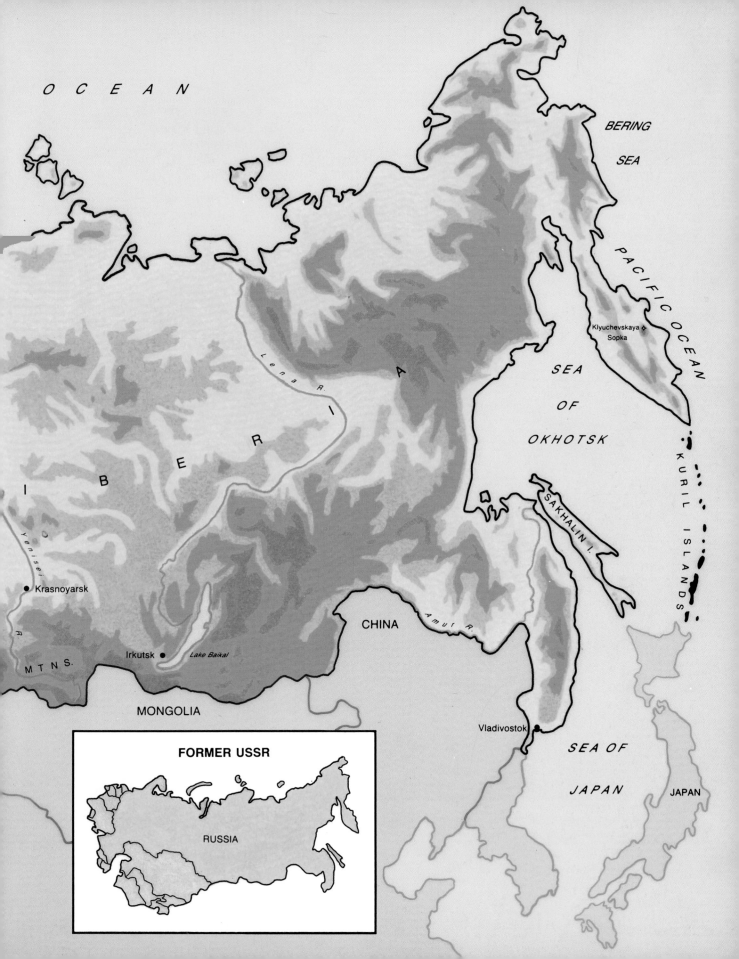

O C E A N

BERING

SEA

PACIFIC OCEAN

Klyuchevskaya
Sopka

SEA

OF

OKHOTSK

KURIL ISLANDS

S   I

B   E   R   I   A

Lena R.

SAKHALIN I.

Yenisei

R.

Krasnoyarsk

CHINA

Amur R.

M T N S.

Irkutsk   Lake Baikal

MONGOLIA

Vladivostok

SEA OF

JAPAN

JAPAN

FORMER USSR

RUSSIA

• *Climate* •

The tundra region that crosses northern Russia has one of the harshest climates on earth, with extremely long, cold winters and brief summers. In the northwest, winds blowing from the Arctic and Atlantic oceans moderate the severe winter weather. Farther east, however, a lack of ocean winds causes frigid temperatures. The belt of taiga that lies south of the tundra is humid and swampy, despite having low rainfall. Winters are cold, and summers are mild and short. St. Petersburg—a city lying at the western edge of the taiga on the Gulf of Finland—averages 16° (–9° C) in winter and 62° (17° C) in summer.

Outdoor walks require heavy clothing when temperatures drop below freezing during Russia's winter months.

A small waterway winds through the lower slopes of southern Siberia's Altai Mountains. In the spring, the hills in this range are green with newly sprouted grass, while taller peaks are still capped with snow.

During autumn, trees near the Gulf of Finland gradually shed their yellow leaves.

The fertile steppes south and southwest of the Ural Mountains are unprotected from the cold winds that sweep down from the north. In late summer, hot and dry winds, called **sukhoveys**, blow dust and topsoil across the open fields of the steppes. In autumn, cold rains turn the steppes into impassable seas of mud. Winter brings snow, bitter cold, and very long, dark nights. Volgograd, a city on the southern steppes, averages 14° (−10° C) in winter and 75° (24° C) in summer. The Caucasus region to the south enjoys mild weather in spring and autumn. A narrow strip along the Black Sea coast enjoys a warm climate with long, sunny summers.

Villagers herd their livestock home from pastures in southern Siberia.

Toxic waste from this pulp mill, located on the shores of Lake Baikal, endangers the lake's unique species of plants and animals.

Saving Lake Baikal

Russian folk songs refer to Lake Baikal as a "glorious and sacred sea." Environmentalists call it the "gem of Siberia." The world's oldest and deepest lake, Baikal holds one-fifth of the earth's total supply of fresh water. The lake has survived for so long because oxygen circulates all the way to the lake's floor —5,315 feet (1,620 meters) at the lowest point. Scientists believe that heat from deep within the earth warms the lake bottom, causing the water to move and to distribute oxygen.

The oxygen-rich, heated water supports more than 2,000 species of plants and animals. At least 1,000 of them are found nowhere else in the world. The rapid growth of industries along the shores of Lake Baikal, however, threatens this unique environment.

In the 1950s, a giant paper and pulp mill began to pour toxic chemicals into the lake. In addition, rivers that flow into Lake Baikal brought in farm fertilizers and other poisonous chemicals. As a result, the chemical balance of Lake Baikal's water changed and now threatens many of its plants and animals.

In the 1980s, Russians campaigned to protect Lake Baikal from further pollution. Activists pressed the Soviet government to install equipment to decrease the amount of waste running into the lake from the paper and pulp factory. The concerns that people raised also stopped plans for the construction of other industrial complexes along the lakeshore.

In the 1990s, the Russian government will either tear down existing factories or will force them to switch to cleaner production processes. With the help of the Russian people, Lake Baikal may remain a glorious sea and a living laboratory.

Shoppers look for bargains at a huge department store in Moscow.

Built on marshland, St. Petersburg became the capital of the Russian Empire in the early 1700s. Czar Peter I (the Great) hired European architects to design the city's royal palaces and public squares.

• Cities •

Moscow, the capital of Russia, lies in the western part of the country. With a population of more than eight million, it is the largest city both in Russia and in the former Soviet Union. In the middle of Moscow is the Kremlin, an old fortress that now serves as the center of government. The onion-shaped domes of St. Basil's Cathedral tower over the vast open spaces of Red Square, which lies outside the eastern wall of the Kremlin. In the rest of this sprawling city, splendid old mansions and

Sparks fly from the machinery at a steel plant in Volgograd. This important industrial hub lies at one end of a canal that links the Volga and Don rivers.

churches compete for space with huge concrete apartment buildings that have been raised during the last 50 years.

According to tradition, Moscow was founded by Prince Yuri Dolgoruky in 1147. For many years, it prospered from trade between southern Russia and Scandinavia (Sweden, Norway, Denmark, and Finland). The Tatars of central Asia overran and destroyed the city in the 13th century. Moscow became the capital of the surrounding region in 1547, when Ivan IV, or Ivan the Terrible, became "czar of all the Russias." Although Czar Peter I (the Great) moved his court and government to St. Petersburg in 1713, the Communists who overthrew the last of the czars moved the capital back to Moscow in 1918.

St. Petersburg—until recently called Leningrad—is Russia's second largest city, with a population of four million. Peter the Great planned and built this city on the Gulf of Finland as a meeting point for Russia and western European nations. For more than 200 years, St. Petersburg was the capital of the Russian Empire, and Russian and European architects were brought here by the czars to build fine palaces, churches, and squares.

Other historic cities in European Russia include Pskov, Yaroslavl, and Novgorod, which dates to the 9th century. Voronezh and Volgograd in the south are important industrial centers. Ekaterinburg (formerly Sverdlovsk), a city of more than one million inhabitants, is the center of a huge mining region east of the Ural Mountains. Nizhni Novgorod (formerly Gorki), Kazan, Samara, and Simbirsk are industrial cities on the banks of the Volga River. Siberia's largest cities are Irkutsk, near the western shore of Lake Baikal, Novosibirsk in south central Siberia, Krasnoyarsk on the Yenisei River, and Vladivostok, a port on the Sea of Japan.

• Russia's Ethnic Heritage •

Russia's population of 148 million includes more than 100 nationalities. Although **Slavs** are a majority in Russia, the nation contains many different ethnic groups. Several of these have their own semi-independent territories that are known as **autonomous republics.**

The largest minorities are the Tatars, the Ukrainians, and the Chuvashes. The Tatars originated in Mongolia and invaded Russia in the 13th century. Ukrainians have intermixed with the Russians for centuries, and a large minority of Russians still lives within independent Ukraine. The Chuvashes, who are related to the Finns, have lived in the northern part of European Russia since the beginning of the country's history. Other groups include Kolmyks, Germans, Chukchi, Ingushi, and Buriats.

Most members of these various ethnic groups speak Russian, an Indo-European tongue that is the

Wearing traditional costumes, Russian dancers and singers perform at a national festival.

Many different ethnic groups live within Russia. These scientists have a central Asian heritage.

After saying a prayer in memory of a loved one, a Russian Orthodox believer lights a candle at a church in St. Petersburg.

Schoolchildren gather outside their apartment complex in Moscow. Students attend classes for an average of 10 years beginning at age 7.

most widely used language within the former borders of the Soviet Union. Russian and Old Church Slavonic, the language of the Russian Orthodox Church, are written in Cyrillic, an alphabet based on the letters of ancient Greek. People from central Asia who are living in Russia speak Turkic languages, and Latvians, Lithuanians, and Estonians speak languages that use the Latin alphabet.

• Religion and Festivals •

Most Russians are members of the Russian Orthodox Church, a branch of the Eastern Orthodox Church. Under Communist rule, the church received no state support, and many Orthodox places of worship were closed. In the late 1980s, however, the Soviet government eased restrictions on religious worship, and many Russian churches reopened. More than 5,000 Orthodox churches now hold services

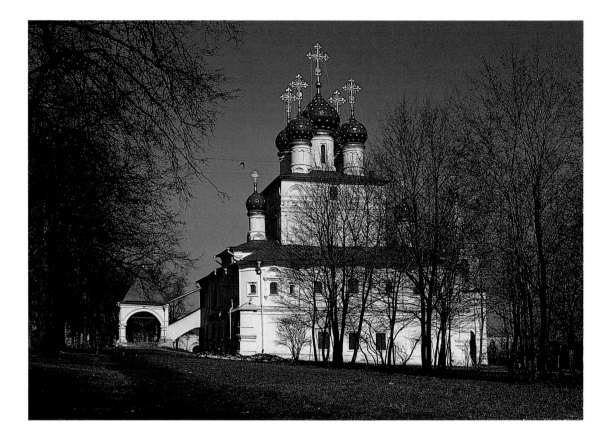

throughout Russia. Other Christian denominations include Lutheranism and Roman Catholicism. Russia's Jewish population numbers more than 500,000.

Easter, observed with midnight services and ornate festivities, is the most important event in the Orthodox calendar. During the Christmas season, which lasts from December 24 until January 6, decorated trees adorn private homes, and Russian children eagerly await presents brought by "Father Frost"—who looks very much like Santa Claus.

Islam, a religion founded in the Middle East, is practiced in areas bordering the former Soviet republics of central Asia. Many Muslims (followers of Islam) in these republics are forming new alliances with Iran, Turkey, and other Middle Eastern states in which Islam is the dominant faith.

Russian Orthodox churches are often topped by brightly colored domes.

A student helps his younger brother to read a Russian textbook. Decades of compulsory education have given nearly all Russians the ability to read and write their native language.

• Health and Education •

The USSR was the first country in the world to offer free health care for all. Although many diseases have been brought under control, the quality of medical facilities declined greatly in the 1970s and 1980s. The rate of infant mortality—the number of babies who die during the first year of life—is still high at 18 per 1,000 births. Life expectancy—70 years—is lower than in most western European countries. An improvement in the Russian economy would allow the government to modernize its hospitals and clinics, to import urgently needed medicines, and to buy new medical equipment.

Under the Soviet government, all Russians had a free education from primary through postsecondary schools. Students were required to finish 10 years of school between the ages of 7 and 17. Russia has more than 900 institutions of postsecondary study. Technical and trade schools train students for work in medicine, teaching, and other professions. Although nearly all Russians can read and write, many graduates will have difficulty finding jobs, since the government no longer guarantees employment.

Although Russia offers government-funded health services, family members often care for the elderly in their homes.

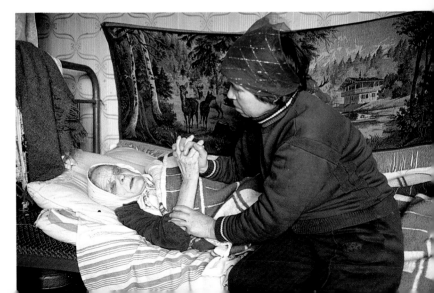

CHAPTER TWO

Russia's Story

Russians, Ukrainians, and Belarussians all belong to the Slavic family of peoples. Originally from central Asia, the Slavs moved westward and settled in European Russia in the 6th century A.D. Slavic towns along the rivers of northern and western Russia prospered from trade with eastern Europe and Scandinavia. But the Slavs, who did not unify their cities, suffered frequent invasions that disrupted their trade.

In the 10th century, the princes of a Slavic state called Rus united the Slavs who lived on the banks of the Dnieper River (now in Ukraine) and in the northern part of European Russia. Kiev, the largest city of Ukraine, became the capital of Rus. Kievan Rus maintained trade with Scandinavia and Europe and came into contact with the Byzantine Empire to the south.

In 988, Vladimir, a prince of Kievan Rus, forced his subjects to be baptized into the Eastern Orthodox Church, the faith of the Byzantine Empire.

The onion-shaped domes and golden crosses of a Russian Orthodox church rise above Moscow.

3

Icons are paintings on wood or metal that usually have a religious theme. Subjects for icon artists include the birth of Jesus (right) and scenes from the life of the Virgin Mary (below right).

Vladimir chose Orthodoxy at a time when the rest of Europe was practicing Roman Catholicism. The adoption of Orthodoxy isolated the Slavic peoples from western Europe and resulted in the development of a unique culture. Russian architects and painters created churches and **icons** (religious paintings) that were strongly influenced by Byzantine works.

• Tatar Invasion •

For several centuries after Vladimir's death in 1015, Kievan Rus expanded its boundaries and successfully fought off the nomadic Asian peoples who were moving across Europe. In 1242, Kiev fell to the Tatars, a warlike people from central Asia. The Tatars, who burned Kiev to the ground, occupied Rus for more than 250 years, cutting off the land and its people from Europe.

Under Tatar rule, the center of power shifted away from Kiev. The city of Moscow, which was situated along busy trading routes northeast of Kiev, began to gain wealth and influence. In 1380, an alliance led by the princes of Moscow defeated the Tatars at the Battle of Kulikovo (southwest of Moscow). Prince Ivan III of Moscow (1462–1505) greatly expanded the territory under the city's control and laid the foundation for the Russian Empire that was ruled by a succession of czars.

In the 15th and 16th centuries, the czars united most of the lands surrounding Moscow. Ivan IV (the Terrible), who was crowned czar in 1547, expanded

The Tatar chief Batu Khan conquered Kievan Rus in the 1230s. His realm — called a khanate — was known as the Golden Horde, after the color of his tent and the word orda, which means "camp."

Russia's borders westward to the Baltic region and eastward across northern Asia. By 1725, much of the territory of modern Russia, including Siberia, had come under the rule of the czars.

• The Russian Empire •

In the early 18th century, during the reign of Peter the Great, Russia became an important European power. Peter strengthened Russia's army and navy and defeated Sweden — one of the strongest powers in Europe — in 1702. After his military victories, this energetic czar brought European engineers and architects to Russia to modernize his empire. To underscore his determination to make

Russia's victory in the Battle of Kulikovo in 1380 signaled the end of Tatar rule in Kievan Rus. Thereafter, Russian princes and czars controlled the Russian state. The coat of arms of the czars featured a double eagle. Peter the Great added the naval maps clutched in the birds' beaks and talons.

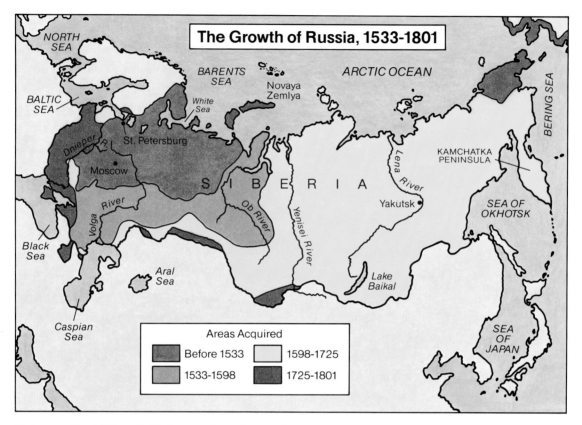

The Growth of Russia, 1533-1801

Areas Acquired

Before 1533   1598-1725
1533-1598   1725-1801

Between the 16th and 18th centuries, the Russian Empire expanded to include the vast Asian lands of Siberia and parts of eastern Europe. Much of the growth occurred in the 1700s, during the reigns of Peter I and Catherine II.

Russia a European state, Peter built St. Petersburg on the Gulf of Finland and moved his capital there from Moscow.

Peter's attempts to modernize Russia did little to help the **serfs** — Russian farm laborers who were the legal property of landowners. During the 18th century, Russian troops put down several serf uprisings. The czars resisted changes that would have helped the serfs and arrested political opponents who called for reforms in government or a representative parliament.

Russia expanded farther into the Baltic and into eastern Europe during the reign of Catherine II (the

Great, 1762–1796). Catherine's armies conquered parts of Poland, Byelorussia (modern Belarus), and Ukraine. In 1812, the French emperor Napoleon Bonaparte and his armies attacked Russia and took Moscow. After the Russian armies abandoned and set fire to Moscow, Napoleon retreated to the west, losing more than 90 percent of his troops in the process.

After driving out the French, Russia expanded southward into Georgia, Azerbaijan, Armenia, Uzbekistan, Kazakhstan, and Tajikistan. In 1891, workers finished the Trans-Siberian Railroad, which connected Europe with Russia's eastern Asian territories. By the end of the 19th century, the Russian czars ruled one of the largest empires in the world.

• *War and Revolution* •

Despite its advances, Russia in the early 20th century was still backward by most European standards. Russian **peasants** (rural laborers) still lived in poverty, and the empire's workers suffered harsh conditions in factories and mines. The government headed by Czar Nicholas II made little effort to improve the lives of ordinary Russians. In 1905, violent demonstrations swept the country. To meet the popular demands, Nicholas agreed to create a legislature called the Duma.

The Duma gradually gained power at the expense of the czar, and in 1910 the government passed some land reform measures that increased farm production and food exports. Revolutionary activity, however, did not stop. Opponents of the regime known as **socialists** were organizing workers in the cities and calling for an end to the Russian monarchy. The government responded to the unrest by imprisoning and sometimes executing revolutionaries.

Throughout the history of the Russian Empire, the majority of the population lived and worked on large farming estates that belonged to wealthy Russian nobles.

Meanwhile, many European nations were preparing for war. Britain, France, and Russia formed an alliance to stop German expansion. Russia, however, was not prepared for World War I (1914–1918), a long and costly conflict in which the empire suffered devastating military defeats. These setbacks—along with food shortages in the cities—prompted riots in St. Petersburg in February 1917. When government troops refused to fire on the demonstrators, the czarist government collapsed. Nicholas II abdicated (resigned), and the Duma took control of the empire.

The Duma formed a temporary government and prepared for the election of an assembly that would write a Russian constitution. But continuing military defeats and food shortages weakened the government. In November 1917, a small group of revolutionaries called Communists gathered support among workers and sailors in St. Petersburg. Led by Vladimir Lenin, the Communists overthrew the government by force.

• The USSR and Stalin •

The revolutionaries closed down newspapers, prohibited political activity, and had many of their opponents imprisoned or shot. Lenin's government took over banks, stores, factories, and country estates, declaring that all property now belonged to the workers. In March 1918, the Communist government signed a peace treaty with Germany. In the same year, Lenin moved his capital to Moscow.

The Communists still faced organized opposition. In 1918, a civil war broke out that plunged the country into violence and famine. After three years of fighting, the Communists defeated foreign and czarist armies and extended their control to most of the territory belonging to the old Russian Empire.

Born in 1870, the Communist leader Vladimir Lenin directed the 1917 Russian Revolution and later founded the Union of Soviet Socialist Republics (USSR). Using harsh measures, he silenced opponents, abolished private property, and extended state control to private businesses and farms. Lenin died in 1924, and Joseph Stalin succeeded him.

The Communist government declared the founding of the Union of Soviet Socialist Republics (USSR) in 1922. This state included Russia, Ukraine, Byelorussia, and smaller republics in the Caucasus region and in central Asia. The Communists seized property in these republics and forced local governments to follow the policies set by the central Soviet government in Moscow.

After Lenin's death in 1924, Joseph Stalin, a Communist official from Georgia, took power. Ruthless and ambitious, Stalin had many of his former colleagues put on trial and then executed. He sent other opponents to prison camps in Siberia.

In the late 1920s, Stalin began to **collectivize** agriculture. Estates were taken from the landowners and put into the hands of Soviet **collective farms**, which raised crops to sell back to the government. It set prices and distributed food to the cities. By the late 1930s, however, the system was already breaking down. The collectivized farmers were not interested in working hard on land that did not belong to them. Crop yields dropped, and Russia was forced to import huge amounts of food.

As the agricultural sector declined, Stalin started a massive drive to industrialize the Soviet Union. Workers—many of them slave laborers—built giant dams, dug enormous canals, and constructed huge tractor plants. Within a few years, the Soviet Union was a major industrial power.

Farmers harvest beets on a collective farm near Moscow. Stalin's collectivization program created huge agricultural estates by taking over and combining smaller, privately owned farms. Workers ran the collectives, selling their crops to the Soviet government and receiving in return a portion of the food as wages.

• *World War II* •

As Stalin reshaped Russia, the rest of Europe was preparing for another conflict. Under the Nazi leader Adolf Hitler, Germany was building up its armed forces and taking over neighboring countries. In 1939, the Soviet Union signed the **Molotov-Ribbentrop Pact** with Germany. The two nations

WONDER HOW LONG THE HONEYMOON WILL LAST?

A *cartoon shows Stalin* (right) *as the happy bride on the arm of his groom, the German leader Adolf Hitler. The drawing appeared in 1939, soon after the USSR and Germany signed the Molotov-Ribbentrop Pact.*

agreed not to attack one another or to interfere in one another's internal politics. Stalin signed the treaty knowing that his country needed time to prepare for the coming war with Germany.

World War II (1939–1945) broke out when German forces invaded Poland in September 1939. Two years later, German tanks rolled into western Russia. Despite the USSR's rapid military buildup, the Soviet forces were caught by surprise. Their weak resistance allowed Germany to conquer most of European Russia.

To continue the production of weapons, Soviet factories were dismantled and moved to eastern Russia. The USSR's Red Army burned villages and fields to deprive the Germans of food. After four bitter years of fighting, in which more than 20 mil-

During World War II (1939–1945), which Russians know as the Great Patriotic War, women kept Russian factories and farms in operation. Here, a dedicated worker turns the wheel of a combine harvester under a sign that urges farmers to produce more wheat.

lion Soviet soldiers and civilians died, German forces retreated from Russia, leaving many of the country's farms and cities in ruins.

• *Khrushchev to Gorbachev* •

Although Stalin had transformed the Soviet Union into an industrial power, his policies had also weakened the nation's economy. His successor, Nikita Khrushchev, attempted to modernize the Soviet system. But Khrushchev's liberal policies threatened the secure jobs of powerful Communist officials. They forced him to resign in 1964.

After World War II ended in 1945, Soviet leaders maintained a state of military preparation. Frequent parades of the Soviet army and navy showed the government's determination to strengthen its armed forces.

Leonid Brezhnev ruled the Soviet Union after Khrushchev and made little effort to reform the Soviet economic or political systems. During the 1960s and 1970s, as the economy stagnated, ordinary Russians saw their standard of living slowly decline.

With guaranteed employment, Russians had little reason to work hard. Farmers left crops to rot in the fields, and food became scarce in the cities. Russia's abundant resources—including natural gas, oil, diamonds, and gold—were sold abroad so that food could be bought from foreign countries. By the time Brezhnev died in 1982, the USSR was nearly bankrupt.

Mikhail Gorbachev, who became the Soviet Union's leader in 1985, understood that economic and political reforms were necessary for the Soviet Union's survival. The country needed restructuring—**perestroika**, as Gorbachev called it in Russian. Some private ownership of business had to be allowed, and the party bureaucrats would have to give up some of their power.

This pipeline in Siberia transports natural gas to populated areas of Russia.

While campaigning in 1990, Boris Yeltsin talked to auto-workers in Tatarstan, the autonomous republic established for the Tatars. In 1992, citizens of Tatarstan voted for a change that would allow their region to develop separate relations with other nations without Moscow's approval.

If perestroika were to succeed, people would have to be able to publicly discuss and criticize the system. This new policy of openness was known as **glasnost.** For the first time in 70 years, the press was allowed some independence. Open elections were held in Russia, and non-Communist representatives were voted into a new Russian parliament.

• *The Rebirth of Independent Russia* •

Boris Yeltsin, who served as a delegate to the Russian parliament, became the leader of a Russian independence movement during Gorbachev's term. Yeltsin demanded open elections and a market economy that would allow businesses to make a profit. A dynamic speaker, Yeltsin quit the Communist party and, in the summer of 1991, won Russia's first democratic election for president.

At the same time, perestroika had not relieved inefficiency and shortages of goods. The illegal **black market**, in which people sold goods at high prices for profit, was booming. In addition, nationalities throughout the USSR were demanding independence and threatening to break up the Soviet Union. Many conservative Communists called for a return to strict central control.

Economic and political conditions eventually became so unstable that the conservatives took action. On August 19, 1991, several of Gorbachev's colleagues staged a **coup d'état** (swift takeover) of the Soviet government. They promised to restore order, to keep the USSR together, and to improve the economy. These officials ordered Gorbachev's arrest and sent tanks into the streets of Moscow.

Thousands of Moscow residents gathered at the Russian parliament building to resist the coup. President Yeltsin appeared in front of the building and vowed to defend democracy. An attempt by the

Waiting in long lines to buy consumer goods and food — in this case milk — is a common part of Russian life.

military to storm the building failed, and the coup collapsed.

The coup's failure marked the end of the USSR. The Russian parliament banned the Communist party's activities and took over the offices that once belonged to the Soviet administration. Lacking an official role, Gorbachev resigned. The white, blue, and red flag of Russia replaced the flag of the Soviet Union over the Kremlin in Moscow.

In December, Yeltsin met with the presidents of Belarus and Ukraine. The three leaders agreed to form the Commonwealth of Independent States, which most of the central Asian republics of the old USSR later joined. Instead of a central government, the commonwealth loosely coordinates military and economic affairs among its members.

On August 20, 1991, civilians and soldiers (right) stood shoulder to shoulder at barricades in front of the Russian parliament building. At that time, conservative Communists were trying to overthrow the Soviet president and to reestablish central control over the Soviet republics. The actions of Russians to stop the attempted overthrow led to the collapse of the entire Soviet system.

The white-blue-red Russian flag now flies over the Kremlin in Moscow. The center of government under the czars as well as the Communists, the Kremlin continues to be the hub of administrative activity for independent Russia.

• An Uncertain Future •

Although Russia had won its fight for independence, the struggle for economic survival had just begun. To create a market economy, Yeltsin freed prices in January 1992. The sudden doubling and tripling of prices for food and consumer goods caused extreme hardship for most Russians. Shortages of food and clothing still force shoppers to stand in long lines at Russian stores. Some obsolete businesses have been allowed to close down, and workers are no longer guaranteed employment. If the government freely allows emigration, many Russians may leave.

In addition to its economic woes, Russia is experiencing divisive ethnic tensions. Some nationalities are demanding further independence, a situation that could split the country into rival territories and bring open conflict. Russia also must reach an agreement with Ukraine and other commonwealth members on the future of the former Soviet armed forces and on nuclear weapons.

Despite these problems, Russia can benefit from its large and skilled labor force, its educated professional class, and its enormous resources. If the new Russian government can manage to provide food and economic stability to its people, Russia will emerge again as one of the world's great powers.

CHAPTER THREE

Making a Living in Russia

U nder Communist rule, Russia's economy was under tight government control. The Soviet state owned all property and businesses and set **quotas** (production goals) for Russian farms and factories. Workers were guaranteed jobs, and their pay was fixed by the state.

In the early 1980s, however, the economy and living standards of Russia began to decline. Soviet bureaucrats mismanaged state-owned businesses, and the system of distributing goods broke down, causing severe shortages. Workers, who had little incentive to work hard and to produce more, were often absent from their jobs. The illegal black market encouraged workers and managers to steal goods and to bribe officials to ignore their activities.

Schoolchildren gather carrots from a field near the southern Siberian city of Krasnoyarsk. Shortages of farm machinery often make it necessary for city dwellers of all ages to spend time harvesting crops.

A fallen statue of Joseph Stalin lies in a Moscow park. After the Communist party's hold on power ended in 1991, protesters toppled hundreds of iron and concrete memorials to Communist leaders.

Mikhail Gorbachev's resignation in December 1991 put Boris Yeltsin and his advisers in charge of the Russian economy. Yeltsin wants to return all factories, stores, and land to private hands. He has lifted price controls so that businesses are able to make a profit from goods they produce. If these reforms are successful in creating a market economy, they may address the hardships caused by food lines, unemployment, empty shelves, gas shortages, criminal activity, and fear of famine.

• Manufacturing •

Russia contains some of the world's largest steel mills, automobile and truck factories, and chemical plants. Industrial suburbs made up of new factory complexes circle Moscow and several other Russian cities. St. Petersburg is a major shipbuilding center. Cities along the Volga and in western Russia produce electrical equipment, heavy machinery, construction materials, and railroad cars.

Since the late 1980s, some of Russia's most inefficient factories have ceased to operate. In many of the plants that remain open, Russian managers have not stayed in touch with new developments in factory technology, such as the use of robots. With outdated equipment and shortages of raw materials, factories have difficulty competing with firms in European and Asian countries.

Russia has encouraged foreign countries to invest in and modernize its many manufacturing plants. The sale of industrial concerns to private owners may help to streamline these businesses, and **joint ventures** with foreign firms may provide new jobs to the growing number of unemployed factory workers.

Many Russian industries, such as this machine-tool factory in Moscow, suffer from outdated production methods and obsolete equipment. If modernized, a large number of Russian plants could manufacture high-quality goods.

The lack of computers in Russian factories forces some plant managers to draw up production schedules with pen and paper.

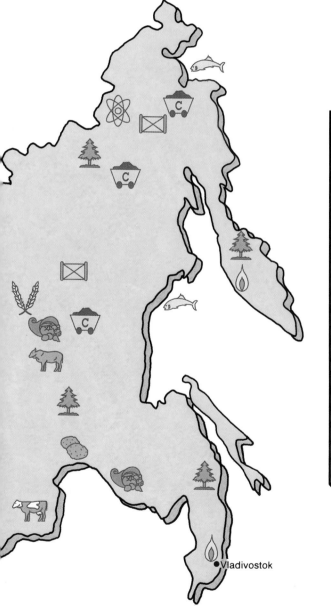

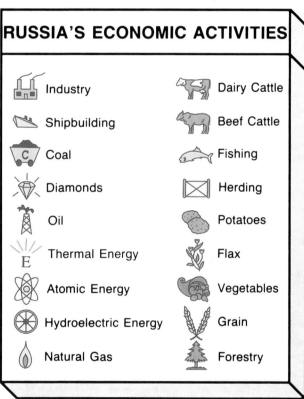

RUSSIA'S ECONOMIC ACTIVITIES

Industry

Shipbuilding

Coal

Diamonds

Oil

Thermal Energy

Atomic Energy

Hydroelectric Energy

Natural Gas

Dairy Cattle

Beef Cattle

Fishing

Herding

Potatoes

Flax

Vegetables

Grain

Forestry

Vladivostok

Rows of turbines power this hydroelectric station in Siberia.

• Mining and Energy •

Russia is extremely rich in oil, natural gas, and gold. It has huge deposits of coal and iron ore (an important ingredient of finished steel), as well as reserves of chromium, titanium, molybdenum, nickel, and other important industrial minerals. These metals and fuels exist mainly in the Urals and in Siberia. The harsh climatic conditions in these regions and the outdated methods used to extract minerals have led to a sharp drop in output. Developers have planned joint ventures to tap oil and gas in the vast Siberian oil fields. Without further investment, however, the production of most raw materials and fuels in Russia will continue to decline.

Russia maintains the hydropower stations that were built on the Volga and Don rivers during the Soviet era. In many cities, oil and hydropower have replaced coal as the fuel for home heating and electricity. Geothermal energy from hot underground water drives several new Russian power plants. Nuclear power stations, built in past decades, are of poor design and lack needed spare parts. Many Russians believe these plants could become dangerous to operate.

Workers use heavy machinery to extract coal from a huge open-pit mine in Siberia. Russia has many large deposits of coal, oil, and natural gas but needs new foreign investment to exploit them.

A *laborer feeds calves on a collective farm near Moscow. The Russian government is breaking up some rural collectives and selling the land and equipment to private farmers.*

• Agriculture •

Although Russia possesses vast areas of fertile land, the country's collective farms have suffered from inefficiency, harsh weather, and a poor distribution system. Government quotas for production were set too high, and the prices the government paid for crops were too low. As a result, farmers had little incentive to modernize their farms or to buy new equipment. The consequences have included declining harvests in the 1980s and early 1990s. Russia has been importing vast amounts of grain to meet demand.

Russia's major crops are grains—such as barley, wheat, corn, oats, and rye. Sugar beets and potatoes are important vegetable crops. Tea is a common crop in the Caucasus region. Sheep, pigs, and cattle are raised in European Russia and in the southern, warmer regions of Siberia. Some northern peoples, such as the Chukchi, herd reindeer to provide meat.

To improve its agriculture, Russia needs to build a new distribution system that will efficiently transport harvested crops to markets. To achieve this, the Russian government has ended quotas and is encouraging wholesalers to supply food to private shops in the cities. Private ownership of land and open markets may help production and reduce the country's dependence on food imports.

• Forestry and Fishing •

Russia's vast stands of pine and birch are among the country's most valuable natural resources. Much of the forested land, however, lies far from the transportation network, causing difficulty in bringing cut trees to mills and ports. Northwestern Russia, from St. Petersburg to the White Sea (an arm of the Barents Sea), is the nation's most productive timber-producing area. Paper, pulp, and other wood products are shipped from this region to the sawmills and port facilities of Arkhangelsk, which lies near the White Sea on Russia's northern seacoast.

Fishing has long been an important economic activity in Russia. Fleets in the Baltic Sea, an arm of the Atlantic Ocean, and in the White Sea net cod, herring, and salmon. Sturgeon in the Caspian Sea lay the salty eggs that are processed into caviar, an important export food. Russian fishing boats also ply the Pacific and Atlantic oceans.

Many Russians grow their food on small, privately owned plots near their homes. Here, a railroad employee (top) *picks potatoes and a housewife* (bottom) *feeds her flock of chickens.*

Birches are hardy, deciduous (leaf-shedding) trees that thrive in Russia's cold northern climate. Forests of evergreen and deciduous trees cover much of the country and offer plentiful raw material to the nation's lumber industry.

Russian fishing crews tow a wide-mouthed net along the floor of the Pacific Ocean in search of fish. After the net is closed, onboard machines reel in the catch.

What's Next for Russia?

The breakup of the Soviet Union in 1991 did not create clear political and national territories. Instead, Russia contains a mixture of ethnic groups that live within artificially drawn borders. Many of its autonomous republics desire partial or complete independence from Russian rule.

The country's relations with other parts of the old USSR are further complicated by the fact that Russians are a large minority population in many of these new nations. Within Russia itself, many ethnic groups originally came from the other 14 former Soviet member-republics.

From a wharf in the Russian port of St. Petersburg, friends gaze at a sunset over the Gulf of Finland, an arm of the Baltic Sea. Trade with Europe by way of this strategic waterway may be one of the keys to Russia's economic future.

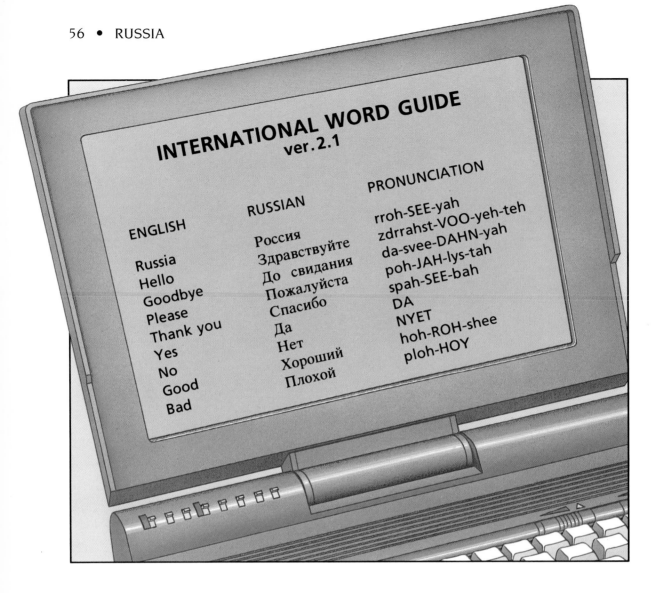

INTERNATIONAL WORD GUIDE
ver. 2.1

ENGLISH	RUSSIAN	PRONUNCIATION
Russia	Россия	rroh-SEE-yah
Hello	Здравствуйте	zdrrahst-VOO-yeh-teh
Goodbye	До свидания	da-svee-DAHN-yah
Please	Пожалуйста	poh-JAH-lys-tah
Thank you	Спасибо	spah-SEE-bah
Yes	Да	DA
No	Нет	NYET
Good	Хороший	hoh-ROH-shee
Bad	Плохой	ploh-HOY

The future of the Russian economy is also in doubt. Yeltsin's market reforms may not solve the country's problems. Food shortages continue, road and rail networks are crumbling, and the value of the ruble, the Russian currency, continues to fall. Increasing unemployment may also cause public unrest, leading to demands for a return to the state-run economy that provided a low but stable standard of living for most citizens.

Foreign trade may help Russia to gain needed hard currency from abroad. Kaliningrad, a harbor city between Lithuania and Poland on the Baltic

Sea, provides cargo ships with a year-round, ice-free port. An agreement between Lithuania and Russia will allow Russia to use rail lines across Lithuania for the transportation of Russian exports to Kaliningrad.

With its vast natural and human resources, Russia may be able to repair its damaged economy. But it will take time, good leadership, and help from abroad to improve conditions and to let the new Russian democracy develop in a peaceful manner.

Buildings in a St. Petersburg square (above) *display decorations that date to the time of the Russian czar Peter the Great. A Russian boy peers from the door of a passenger train* (below) *that connects St. Petersburg with other major cities in Russia.*

FAST FACTS ABOUT RUSSIA

Total Population	148 million
Ethnic Mixture	82 percent Russian 4 percent Tatar 3 percent Ukrainian 1 percent Chuvash
CAPITAL and Major Cities	MOSCOW, Vladivostok, St. Petersburg, Volgograd, Ekaterinburg, Novosibirsk, Nizhni Novgorod, Krasnoyarsk
Major Languages	Russian, Turkic
Major Religions	Russian Orthodoxy, Islam
Year of inclusion in USSR	1922
Status	Fully independent state; took over USSR's seat in the United Nations; founding member of the Commonwealth of Independent States

autonomous republic: one of the semi-independent areas in Russia that were set up to allow ethnic minorities a measure of self-government. Some of these republics are now claiming full independence from the Russian government.

black market: an informal—and often illegal—system of exchanging goods. The black market operates outside of the state-owned distribution system and usually charges high prices.

collectivize: to force private farmers to give up their land and to join collective farms owned by the state.

collective farm: a large agricultural estate worked by a group. The workers usually received a portion of the farm's harvest as wages. On a Soviet collective farm, the central government owned the land, buildings, and machinery.

Commonwealth of Independent States: a union of 11 former Soviet republics that was created by the leaders of Russia, Belarus, and Ukraine in December 1991. The commonwealth has no formal constitution and functions as a loose economic and military association.

Communist: a person who supports Communism —an economic system in which the government owns all farmland and the means of producing goods in factories.

coup d'état: French words meaning "blow to the state" that refer to a swift, sudden overthrow of a government.

glasnost: the Russian name for a policy that eased restrictions on writing and speech.

This McDonald's restaurant opened in Moscow in the late 1980s, thanks to the policy of perestroika, which allowed some foreign firms to establish private businesses in the capital.

icon: a small wooden panel, painted with a religious image, that is common in Russian Orthodox churches, homes, and monasteries.

industrialize: to build and modernize factories for the purpose of manufacturing a wide variety of consumer goods and machinery.

*A **set of statuettes—fashioned after traditional Russian folk art—**depicts Russian and former Soviet leaders, including Mikhail Gorbachev (second from right), **who spearheaded glasnost and perestroika.***

joint venture: an economic partnership between a locally owned business and a foreign-owned company.

Molotov-Ribbentrop Pact: a political agreement negotiated by Vyacheslav Molotov of the Soviet Union and Joachim von Ribbentrop of Germany. Signed in 1939, the agreement said that the two nations would not attack one another or interfere with one another's military and political activities.

peasant: a small landowner or landless farm worker.

perestroika: a policy of economic restructuring introduced in the late 1980s. Under perestroika, the Soviet state allowed small private businesses to form and loosened its control of industry and agriculture.

This grape vendor belongs to the Slavic family of peoples, an ancient ethnic group that now lives throughout Russia and eastern Europe.

quota: the government-set amount of factory goods or food that a group is told to produce.

Russian Empire: a large kingdom that covered present-day Russia as well as areas to the west and south. It existed from roughly the mid-1500s to 1917.

serf: a rural worker under the feudal landowning system, which tied people to a farming estate for life. Serfs had few rights and owed their labor and a large portion of their harvest to the landowner.

Slav: a member of an ethnic group that originated in central Asia and later moved into Russia and eastern Europe.

socialist: a person who favors government ownership of property and a centrally planned economy.

steppe: a level, treeless plain that dominates the landscape of southern Russia.

sukhovey: a hot, dry summer wind that blows across the steppes of western and southern Russia.

taiga: a coniferous (evergreen) forest that extends from the Gulf of Finland across northern Russia to eastern Siberia.

tundra: an arctic region of treeless plains and permanently frozen soil that crosses the extreme north of Russia.

Union of Soviet Socialist Republics (USSR): a large nation in eastern Europe and northern Asia that consisted of 15 member-republics. It existed from 1922 to 1991.

Agriculture, 7, 32–36, 38, 42–43, 49, 52, 61
Architecture, 20–21, 26, 30–31, 57–59
Arctic Ocean, 12–13, 16
Atlantic Ocean, 16, 52
Baikal, Lake, 13, 18–19, 21
Baltic Sea, 32, 52, 55, 56–57
Brezhnev, Leonid, 38
Caspian Sea, 12–13, 52
Catherine II (the Great), 32–33
Cities, 10–11, 20–21, 38–39, 43–45. See also Moscow; St. Petersburg; Volgograd
Climate, 16–17
Commonwealth of Independent States, 9, 40–41
Communists, 7–8, 21, 25, 34–35, 37, 39–41, 43–44
Demonstrations, 2–3, 8, 33–34, 39, 44
Duma, 33–34
Economy, 8–9, 27, 37–41, 43–53, 54–57
Education, 25, 27
Elections, 8, 34, 39
Energy, 48
Environmental concerns, 13, 18–19
Ethnic groups, 9, 24, 29, 41, 55, 62
Europe, 7, 21, 27, 29–35, 55, 62
Exports, 33, 52, 57
Festivals, 24, 26
Finland, Gulf of, 11–12, 16, 21, 32, 54–55
Fishing, 52–53
Food shortages, 34–35, 38–41, 44, 56
Forestry, 12, 52–53
Germany, 34–37
Gorbachev, Mikhail, 38–40, 44
Health, 27

History, 29–41
  independence, 6–8, 39–41
  1950s to 1980s, 18–19, 37–39
  Russian Empire, 7, 20–21, 30, 31–34
  Stalin era, 35–37
  Tatars, 21, 24, 30–31, 38–39
Hitler, Adolf, 35–36
Imports, 27, 35, 49, 52
Independence, 6–8, 39–41
Industry. See Manufacturing
Ivan IV (the Terrible), 21, 30–31
Japan, 12
Japan, Sea of, 12, 21
Jobs, 27, 34–35, 38, 41, 43–45, 50–51
Khrushchev, Nikita, 37–38
Kievan Rus, 29–31
Kremlin, 6–7, 20, 40–41
Lakes, 13. See also Baikal, Lake
Languages, 24–25, 27
Leningrad. See St. Petersburg

Lenin, Vladimir, 34–35
Life expectancy, 27
Livestock, 13, 16–17, 49, 52
Manufacturing, 7, 18–19, 21, 33, 35–39, 43–45, 53, 60
Maps and charts, 14–15, 32, 46–47, 56–57
Mining, 21, 33, 48–49
Molotov-Ribbentrop Pact, 35–36
Moscow, 6–9, 20–21, 25, 28–30, 32–35, 39–41, 44–45, 49, 60
Mountains, 12, 16. See also Ural Mountains
Natural resources, 9, 38, 48, 52, 57
Pacific Ocean, 12, 52–53
People, 22–23, 24–27, 50–51
  education, 25, 27
  ethnic groups, 9, 24, 29, 41, 55, 62
  health, 27
  languages, 24–25, 27
  religion, 25–26, 28–30
Peter I (the Great), 20–21, 31–32, 57

Fast boats transport passengers on the many canals that criss-cross St. Petersburg.

Political systems, 32, 36, 38–40, 55

Pollution. See Environmental concerns

Population, 24

Ports, 21, 52, 57. See also St. Petersburg

Republics, former Soviet, 8–9, 11–12, 24, 26, 29, 33, 35, 40–41, 55–57

Religion, 25–26, 28–30

Rivers, 12–13, 18–19, 20–21, 29, 48. See also Volga River

Russia
boundaries, size, and location of, 11–13
government of, 6–7, 18–19, 20, 27, 32–35, 37, 39–41, 43, 49, 52, 61
population of, 24

Russian Empire, 7, 20–21, 30, 31–34

St. Petersburg, 13, 16, 20–21, 25, 32, 34, 44, 52, 54–55, 56–57, 63

Scandinavian countries, 11, 21, 29, 31

Seas, 12, 17, 21, 52. See also Baltic Sea; Caspian Sea

Siberia, 8, 12–13, 16–17, 18–19, 21, 31–32, 35, 38, 42–43, 48–49, 52–53, 61

Soviet Union, 7–9, 18–19, 20, 25, 27, 34–40, 43, 55

Sports and recreation, 8, 10–11, 20

Stalin, Joseph, 34–37, 44

Standard of living, 33, 38, 43, 56

Tatars, 21, 24, 30–31, 38–39

Topography, 11–12

Trade, 21, 29–30, 54–55, 56

Transportation, 13, 33, 52, 54–55, 57, 63

Unemployment, 44–45, 56

Union of Soviet Socialist Republics (USSR). See Soviet Union

Ural Mountains, 5, 11, 17, 21, 48

Volga River, 12–13, 21, 45, 48

Volgograd, 9, 17, 21

Warfare, 9, 33–37

World War I, 34

World War II, 9, 35–37

Yeltsin, Boris, 8, 38–41, 44, 56

• *Photo Acknowledgments* •

Photographs are used courtesy of: pp. 1, 9 (right), 13 (left), 17 (top), 20 (right), 22 (top and bottom left), 24 (left), 25 (left and right), 27 (left and right), 35, 40 (top), 44, 45 (left and right), 49, 50 (top and bottom right), 51 (bottom), 52 (bottom), 53 (top), 54, 57 (top and bottom), 59 (top left and right), 60, 61, 62, 63, Jeff Greenberg; p. 2, © SYGMA; pp. 5, 8, 12, 13 (right), 17 (bottom), 18, 50 (bottom left), 51 (top left), 52 (top), 58 (top), 59 (bottom), © Dan Buettner; p. 6, © Shepard Sherbell / SABA; p. 9 (left), © Havlicek / ZEFA, H. Armstrong Roberts / Stock South; pp. 10, 48 (top), © Dieter Blum / Peter Arnold, Inc.; p. 16 (left), © Kenneth Garrett / FPG International; pp. 16 (right), 26, 30 (bottom), 41 (top), Sergej Schachowskoj; pp. 18 (inset), 28, © Galem Rowell / Peter Arnold, Inc.; p. 20 (left), Russell Adams; p. 21, © Michael Reagan / FPG International; p. 23 (top left), © Boyd Norton; p. 23 (top right), Nik Wheeler / *Aramco World*; p. 23 (bottom), © Wolfgang Kaehler; pp. 22 (bottom right), 24 (right), 58 (bottom right), Private Eyes; p. 30 (top), Elvehjem Museum of Art, University of Wisconsin-Madison; pp. 31 (left), 36 (left), Independent Picture Service; p. 33, Mansell Collection; p. 34, Steve Feinstein; p. 36 (right), Mark Sawtelle; p. 37, © Vladimir Pcholkin / FPG International; p. 38, Phillips Petroleum Company; p. 39, © NOVOSTI / Lehtikuva Oy / SABA; p. 41 (bottom), © A. Nogues / SYGMA; pp. 42, 48 (bottom), © Hans J. Buckard / SABA; p. 51 (top right), Lynda Richards / Images; p. 53 (bottom), © David Falconer; p. 58 (bottom left), © Peter Arnold. Maps and charts: pp. 14-15, 46-47, J. Michael Roy; pp. 31 (right), 32, 56, 57, Laura Westlund.

Covers: (Front) Sergej Schachowskoj; (Back) © Dan Buettner.